MW01137803

The Gnome Craft Book

Thomas and Petra Berger

The Gnome Craft Book

Floris Books

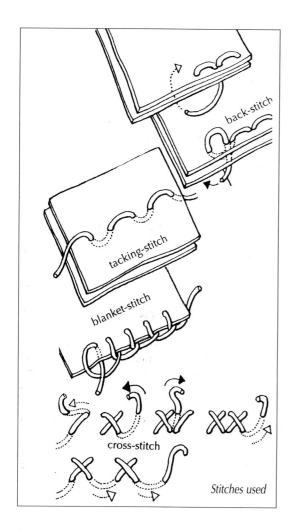

back-stitch

tacking-stitch

blanket-stitch

cross-stitch

Stitches used

Translated by Polly Lawson
Photographs and design by Ernst Thomassen
Patterns by Thomas Berger
Gnome on p. 34 by Francisca Rosenberg
Gnomes on pp.50–58 by Oeke de Ruiter

First published in Dutch in 1999 under the title
Kabouters om zelf te maken
by Christofoor Publishers, Zeist
First published in English in 1999 by Floris Books

© 1999 Thomas and Petra Berger/Uitgeverij Christofoor
This translation © Floris Books, 1999
Second printing 2001

British Library CIP Data available

ISBN 0–86315–300–3

Printed in Belgium

Knitting stitches

stocking stich: 1 row plain, 1 row pearl
ribbed: 1 stitch plain, 1 stitch pearl

Contents

Introduction

Story-telling tradition in many countries has handed down tales of encounters with the little folk' — gnomes, dwarfs, leprechauns or other kinds, depending on the region and surroundings.* All of these are nature spirits, usually found in remote forests and mountains, moors and farmland. Some people even have the gift of seeing them, and say they are like little men not more than two foot tall, with silvery beards and ruddy faces, and are dressed in bright warm clothes, with pointed caps on their heads. It is little figures like these that we shall be describing and making in this book.

For rural communities, it has always been important to work in harmony with the little folk because this leads to prosperity and health. Gnomes traditionally helped the farmer or forester. They worked for the good of plants and animals and practised arts of caring and healing. Some little folk, of course, were mischievous and had to be treated with caution but these were exceptions. If treated well, most gnomes were helpful and generous, repaying kindness a hundredfold.

The craft of making gnome figures therefore echoes a long tradition of giving the nature spirits respect and keeping their presence in mind. Gnome figures can be emblems of our connection with the natural world and remind us how important it is to honour the living spirits of the earth.

In this book we try to show a variety of gnome figures. There are many ways of making them, so you can choose for yourself, taking into account the materials you have available. Some of the figures are easy to make, but others will require more time and, above all, patience.

Some of the figures ares designed to be used as ornaments, others are for playing with. Undoubtedly there are many other ways of designing your figures. We recommend that you do not just copy the models in this book but develop your own ideas.

Sizes and patterns
— An upright hat is included in the given height. You can of course alter the size of the gnome by adjusting the measurements of the pattern.
— For knitted gnomes only the complicated parts of the pattern are shown.
— In practice there may be a discrepancy between the measurements given in the pattern and the finished gnome because of differences in the wire frames and/or stuffing. Before cutting out the pattern measure the material carefully.
— Unless otherwise stated the patterns are the right size. With materials other than felt you need to include an extra 1/2 cm (1/4") around the pattern to make a seam.

Thomas and Petra Berger

---

* A collection of tales of little folk from different regions and countries can be found in *Over the Hills and Far Away,* Floris Books.

Gnomes Made with Felt

Simple felt gnome (5 cm, 2″)

Pieces of felt, unspun sheep's wool.

These little gnomes are ideal for children to play with, and very simple to make. You can leave the bottom open with the unspun wool stuffing showing (see the pattern, Figure 2a).

— Cut out the gnome's cloak. You can either let the cloak run straight down, or round it at the bottom. If you are making several gnomes vary their size by cutting out the pattern in different sizes. Make sure that you do not make the heads too small.
— Sew up the seam of the hood (a) and stitch a gathering-thread at the place shown.
— Tease out some wool before stuffing it into the cloak, and pull the gathering-thread, tying it firmly at the front. Leave a rounded cloak open, or sew up the top front of a square-edged cloak.
— Tease a piece of wool out below the head to make a beard.
— Cut away any extra wool at the bottom to make a flat base.
— For very small children it is better to close the bottom with a piece of felt (see the central circle of the pattern, Figure 2b).
— Reinforce the base with a round piece of card on the inside (Figure 3) before sewing the base on.

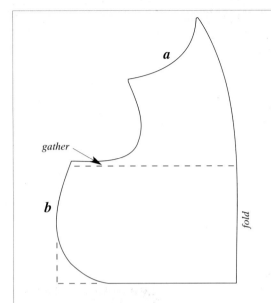

Figure 2a. Pattern for felt gnome open at the base.

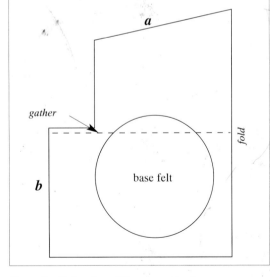

Figure 2b. Pattern for a felt gnome with a base.

Figure 1. Simple gnomes made of felt.

9

Figure 3. Simple gnomes made of felt.

Pencil gnome (8 cm, 3″)

Pieces of felt, coloured pencils, wooden beads (diameter 14 mm, ½″), 2 small beads (diameter 3 mm, ⅛″), about 25 cm (10″) thin wire, adhesive tape.

This makes a good present to hand out at a birthday party.

— Push a piece of wire through the centre of the large bead until it is in the middle of the wire. Hold the bead upright so that the hole in the bead and the wire are both vertical. Bend the wire above the bead, bring it down and twist it several times round the wire at the bottom of the bead to make a neck. Keep the two bits of wire together.
— Cut out felt as in the patterns in Figure 4. Cut a small hole for the neck in the jacket and collar.

Variation
You can also fill this gnome with white or light-coloured knitting-wool. Wind the wool about twenty times around your fingers and stuff the loops into the hood of the doll. Finish off as described above.

Figure 5. Pencil gnomes.

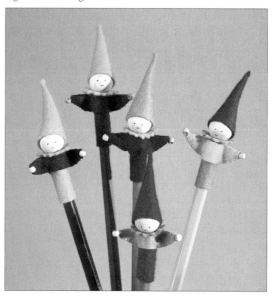

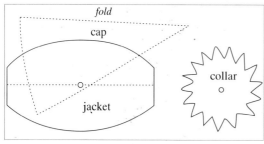

Figure 4. Pattern for pencil gnome.

Thread the collar and then the jacket on to the wire.

— Bend one wire to the right and the other to the left to make the arms. Thread a small bead on to each wire about 2 cm (1") from the neck to make the hands. Bend the wires around the beads and then back to the middle. Twist them together several times (Figure 6).

— Put the doll on the top of the pencil, with the spare wire on either each side of the pencil.

— Attach these wires as firmly as possible to the pencil with adhesive tape (Figure 6). If necessary cut off any surplus wire.

— Cut out a 3 x 3 cm (1¼" x 1¼") piece of felt, glue it around the pencil and the wire.

— Sew up the sleeves of the jacket.

— Sew up the seam of the hat (Figure 4) and glue it on to the head. If you like, draw a face on the gnome.

Flower gnomes (7 cm, 3")

Pieces of felt or thin card
Wooden bead (diameter 2 cm, ¾")
Unspun sheep's wool or carded fleece
Wooden skewer (c. 20 cm, 8" long)

These gnomes love to stand among flowers in a pot. As a treat for children you can also hang soft sweets, dates, figs, large raisins or pieces of cheese on the sticks as well.

— Glue a bead on to the wooden skewers or other thin stick. If the stick is thinner than the hole you can glue some paper round the end of the stick to make it thicker.

— Cut felt or thin card as in the pattern in Figure 8a.

Figure 6. Detail of pencil gnome.

Figure 7. Flower gnomes.

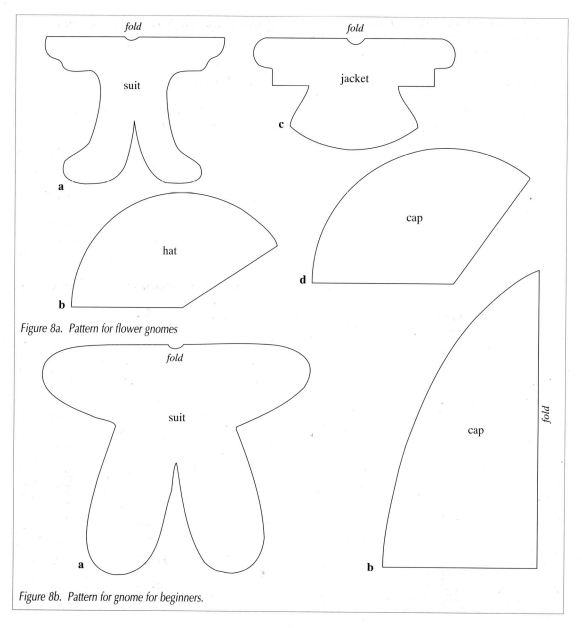

fold

suit

fold

jacket

c

a

hat

cap

d

b

Figure 8a. Pattern for flower gnomes

fold

suit

cap

fold

a

b

Figure 8b. Pattern for gnome for beginners.

— Slip the jacket or the suit on to the stick. Fold the jacket (or suit) over and glue both sides together. The stick will now stand firm.
— Stick the hat on to the bead. The edges will overlap at the back.
— Give the gnome some hair and a beard by gluing teased-out wool on to the bead.
— Draw a face with a pencil.

Figure 9. Detail of gnomes for beginners.

Gnome for beginners (14 cm, 5½")

Pipe-cleaner (26 cm, 10" long) or two short
   pipe-cleaners (13 cm, 5")
Pieces of felt
Plain wooden bead (diameter 24 mm, 1")
Unspun sheep's wool

— Bend a long pipe-cleaner in two, insert and glue the bend into the bead (Figure 18 on p. 20). Allow the glue to dry.
— Cut out the patterns in Figure 8b. The suit is in one piece.
— Push the pipe-cleaner into the neck of the suit.
— Bend the pipe-cleaner into the shape of the gnome's suit and cut the legs off at the right length.
— Wrap a little unspun wool round the arms,

Figure 10. Gnome for beginners.

13

body and legs. This is shown on the left side of Figure 9 (the front part of the suit is not shown in the photograph).

— Sew up the suit.
— Sew up the hat and glue it to the head.
— Give the gnome some unspun wool for hair and a beard.
— Draw a face.

Rose-hip gnome (8 cm, 3")

Pipe-cleaners
Pieces of felt
Plain wooden bead (diameter 18 mm, ³/₄")
2 red beads (diameter 6 mm, ¹/₄")
Soft red material (like cotton or flannel)
Unspun sheep's wool
Piece of card

— Cut out the felt as in Figure 11. Use the soft red material for the large circle. Sew around the edge

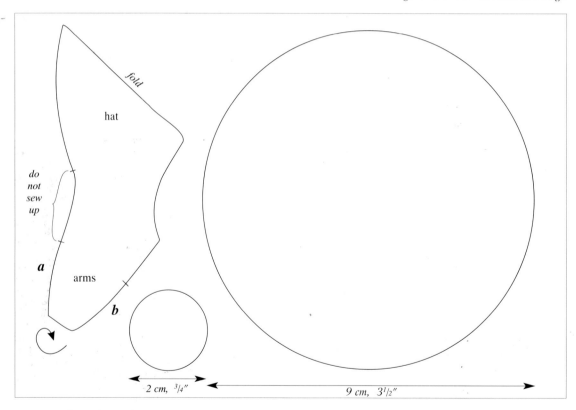

Figure 11. Pattern for rose-hip gnome.

14

using strong thread. Glue the little round disc in the middle of the circle so that the gnome will stand better when finished.

— Place a tuft of unspun wool on the material keeping the piece of card on the inside. Pull the thread and tie firmly. This is the gnome's body.

— Take the large bead, make sure that the hole is vertical, run the pipe-cleaner through the hole and down the back of the head and wind it round the neck to fix the head..

— Take a length (about 8 cm, 3") of pipe-cleaner and glue a little red bead to each end.

— The hat and the arms form one piece. Sew up the hat leaving a bit open which can be secured to the bead.

— Wrap sides a and b of the arms around the pipe-cleaner and sew up the last 15 mm (¹/₂") of each side (Figure 12).

— Glue the hat on to the bead and give the gnome some hair and a beard made from unspun wool.

— Draw a face on the bead.

Figure 12. Detail of rose-hip gnome.

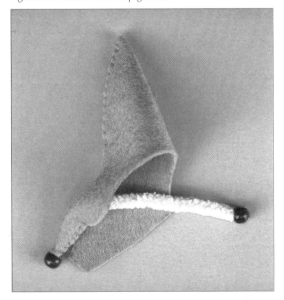

Figure 13. Rose-hip gnome.

15

Figure 14. Finger puppet gnome.

Finger puppet gnome (12 cm, 5")

Pipe-cleaners
Pieces of felt
Pink cotton material
Unspun sheep's wool
Elastic (about 35 mm, 1¹/₂" wide)

— For the head cut out a 10 x 10 cm (4" x 4") piece of pink cotton. Make a firm ball of unspun wool, about 3 cm (1") in diameter, and put it in the middle of the material. Wrap the cotton around the ball and tie it round the neck with strong thread. Cut the bottom off squarely. See that the head has as few folds as possible on one side. This side will be the face (Figure 56b on p. 54).
— Make a tube of elastic which fits easily round a (little) finger. This is the body. Push the spare material from the head into the tube and sew them together. If necessary gather the elastic in a little at the top.
— Figure 16 is the pattern for the felt. Cut the trouser material in the middle as shown. Bend the 12 cm (5") pipe-cleaner in two and lay it on top of the trousers. Fold the trouser legs over each part of the pipe-cleaner and sew them up (Figure 15).
— Sew the shoes on to the trouser legs and bend the feet to the front. Sew the trousers on to the bottom of the piece of elastic, so they hang in front of the finger.
— Take a 10 cm (4") piece of pipe-cleaner and sew the hands on to each end. For the sleeves cut out an 8 x 2 cm (3" x ³/₄") piece of felt, and sew it around the pipe-cleaner.
— Sew up the front part of the smock. Wrap the smock round the body and sew up the back. Slip the arms through the openings of the smock and sew up any openings in order to secure the arms. Gather the top of the jacket at the neck.
— Sew up the hat and secure it to the head. Fold the point of the hat down and secure it.
— Give the gnome a beard of unspun wool and embroider the eyes and mouth.

Figure 15. Detail of finger puppet gnome.

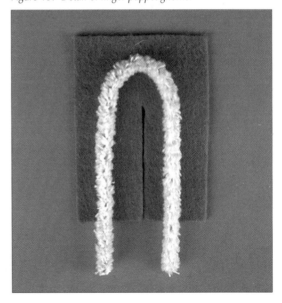

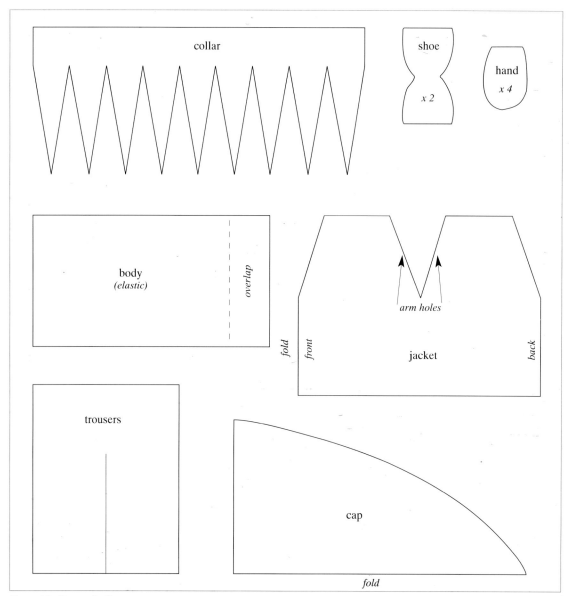

Figure 16. Pattern for finger puppet gnome.

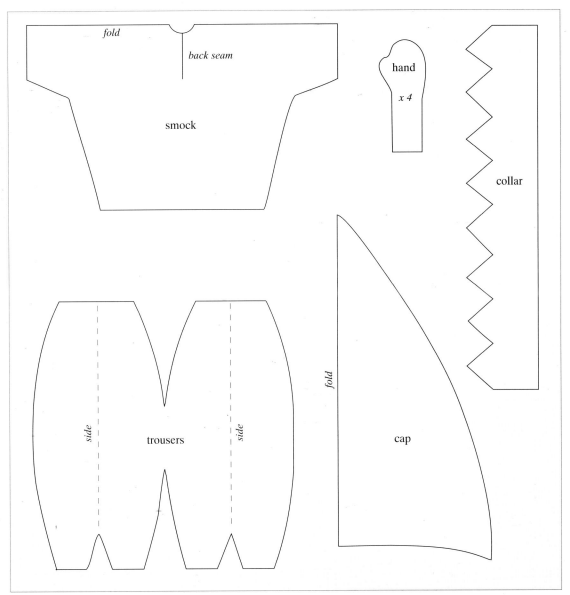

Figure 17. Pattern for gnome with a pipe-cleaner frame.

19

Gnome with a pipe-cleaner frame

(17 cm, 6^1/$_2$")

Pipe-cleaners
Pieces of felt
1 bead (diameter 24 mm, 1")
2 beads (diameter 12 mm, ^{1}/$_2$")
Little beads for decoration
Unspun sheep's wool

— Bend a long pipe-cleaner (26 cm, 10") in two and glue the fold into the thick bead. You can also use two short pipe-cleaners.
— Twist a second pipe-cleaner at right angles to the first pipe-cleaner, just below the bead (Figure 18). Cut out the arms and legs according to the pattern (Figure 17).

Figure 18. Detail of pipe-cleaner frame.

— The pattern in Figure 17 on page 19 is for the clothes.
— Cut out the trouser legs. They should reach the armpits. Wrap them around the legs and sew them up. Sew the other seams of the trousers together.
— Sew the two halves of each hand together and sew them on to the ends of the pipe-cleaner arms.
— Put the smock on the gnome's shoulders and sew up the sleeves and the back. The sleeves should cover the wrists.
— Put the collar around the gnome's neck and secure it.
— Decorate the collar and the smock with embroidery and a few beads.
— Sew the pointed hat together. Glue some unspun wool on to the head and chin to make hair and a beard. Then glue the hat on to the head.
— For feet glue a little bead on to each end of the pipe-cleaners.

Variation
Beads (diameter about 12 and 5 mm, ^{1}/$_2$" and ^{1}/$_4$")
Thin wire

Figure 21 shows some individual little gnomes, which are easier to make, especially as it is easier to make the frame for very small gnomes with wire rather than pipe-cleaners (Figure 20). For the clothes make the patterns in Figure 17 a little smaller.

Figure 19. Gnomes with pipe-cleaner frames.

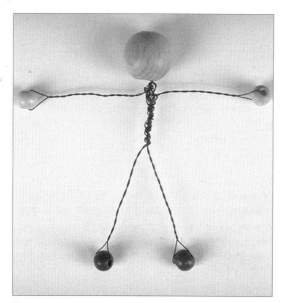

Figure 20. Frame.

Figure 21. Gnomes wrapped in yarn.

Gnomes wrapped in yarn
(10–12 cm, 4-5")

Pieces of felt
Thin wire
Beads (diameter 14 and 6 mm, ¹/₂" and ¹/₄")
Knitting wool
Unspun sheep's wool

These gnomes (Figure 22) have a frame of thin wire.

— Take a piece of wire and put it into the large bead to make the head. Bend the wire around the bead, making sure that the hole in the bead is vertical. Twist the two parts of the wire together under the bead to make a neck (Figure 20).
— For the arms, bend the two wires to the left and right. Slip a little bead on to each wire and bend the ends of the wires backwards and then twist them together.
— Fold the wires down and put another bead on to each. Turn the wires up again and twist the remaining wires round each other to make the body.
— Wind the yarn round the arms and legs until they are of the desired thickness. For this you can use either one or several colours.
— Fasten the wire.

Hat
Give the gnome either a knitted hat or a felt hat as you wish.
— For the knitted hat cast on 14 stitches. Knit stocking stitch with No. 14 (US # 0) needles. After the fifth row decrease on each side (knit the first 2 and the last 2 stitches together) until all the stitches are finished.

Gnomes wrapped with unspun wool
(12 cm, 5")

Pipe-cleaners or thin wire
Beads (diameter 14-18 mm, ⅝" and 8 mm, ¼")
Dyed unspun wool

These gnomes are ornamental and are not designed for playing with.

— Make a frame of pipe-cleaners or wire as you have already done for previous models, but this time leave a bit of the pipe-cleaner sticking out above the bead (for the hat).
— Tease out the unspun wool into very fine tufts and wind them round the pipe-cleaner or wire. Begin with the hands and feet which you can make a little bigger so that you can twist the wool for the clothes over them. Try to build up the body and the hat, layer by layer. The thinner the wool is, and the more the layers you make, the sturdier the gnome will be.
— Give the gnome some hair and a beard.
— Draw a face on the bead.

Variation
Instead of woollen hands and feet you can glue beads on to the ends of the pipe-cleaners.

Grass elf (21 cm, 8")

3 pipe-cleaners (length 15 cm, 6")
Pieces of felt (of various colours: green, white
*   for the beard)*
Wooden bead (diameter 25 mm, 1")
Unspun wool or cotton wool

— Make the frame of pipe-cleaners as in Figure 18 on page 20.
— The pattern in Figure 23 is for the clothes.
   The gnome has trousers which reach from his armpits to his feet. The trousers consist of two separate trouser legs. Sew the trouser legs around the legs of the frame. Sew the legs on top of each other where they meet at the hips. Leave 3 cm (1¼") of the pipe-cleaner sticking out below the trouser legs to fix the shoes.
— Pull the smock over the head with the slit at the back. Sew up the slit, the sleeves and the side of the smock. Leave 1 cm (½") of the pipe-cleaner sticking out of the sleeves to make the hands.
— Sew each half of the hands and shoes together, and push them on to the ends of the pipe-cleaner. Secure them to the sleeves and trouser legs with a few stitches.

Figure 22. Gnomes wrapped in yarn.

leg

x 2

beard

cap

fold

jacket

shoe

x 4

x 4

fold

Figure 23. Pattern for grass elf.

Figure 24. Grass elf.

— Sew the hat together and fill it with a little unspun wool or cotton wool. Pull the hat over the head. The longer part of the hat is at the back. Sew the hat on to the back at armpit height. If necessary glue the hat to the forehead. The beard and hair are one piece. Sew it on to the hat.
— Finally draw or paint a face with watercolours.

Tree gnome (15 cm, 6″)

Pieces of felt
Knitting wool
Knitting needles No. 9 (US # 4)
Unspun sheep's wool or cotton wool
Pipe-cleaner (length 12 cm, 5″)
Piece of thin card

— Knit the head. Cast on 20 stitches, knit 12 rows, 1 plain 1 purl, and cast off. Fold the knitted piece in two. Sew up the side seams and gather the bottom. Fill the head with unspun wool or cotton wool.
— Cut out the clothes as in the pattern of Figure 26a.
— For the body take a 10 x 7 cm (4″ x 3″) piece of felt and sew it into a tube 7 cm (3″) long. Gather the top a little and sew the head on to it.
— Cut two slits at shoulder height for the arms.
— The arms and hands are in one piece. Sew up the bottom with the pipe-cleaner inside. Push the arms through the two slits in the tube and secure them to it.
— Sew the pointed hat together, and sew it on to the head.
— Make the hair as follows: With a crochet hook draw a woollen thread through one of the stitches at the edge of the face to make a loop which sticks out. Pass the two ends of the thread through the loop and pull tight (Figure 26a).

— Sew a double woollen yarn irregularly around the bottom of the body to make it look like bark.
— Fill the tube with unspun wool or cotton wool.
— Cut out a disc of card that is smaller than the felt disc and glue it to the felt disc. Sew the disc on to the bottom of the tube so that the gnome will stand better.
— Finish by embroidering the face.

Figure 25. Tree gnomes.

26

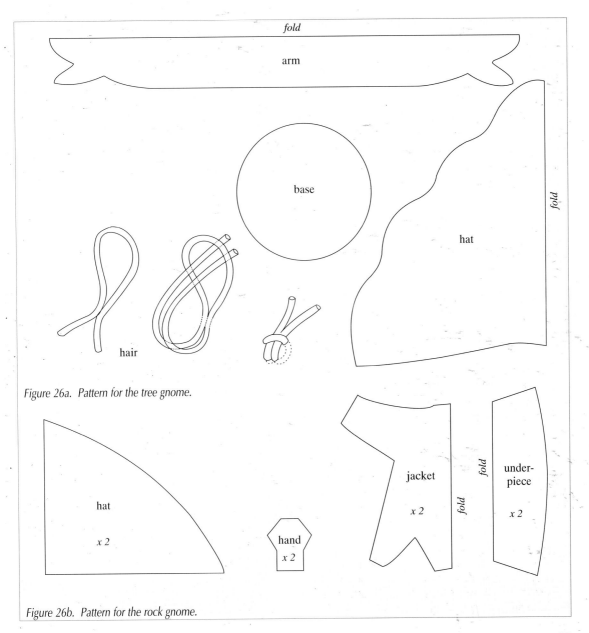

fold

arm

base

fold

hat

hair

Figure 26a. Pattern for the tree gnome.

hat

x 2

hand
x 2

jacket

x 2

fold

fold

under-
piece

x 2

Figure 26b. Pattern for the rock gnome.

Wooden Gnomes

Wooden dolls can be bought in various sorts and sizes, with cylindrical or cone-shaped bodies.

Larger wooden dolls sometimes have a hole in the bottom so that they can be used as finger puppets. When you are buying them make sure that the heads are smooth, round and have no nicks in them.

You can also make a doll from a cork and a large bead.

Taper the cork at one end (Figure 27) and make a hole there with a cocktail stick. Glue the stick into the hole. Glue the bead on to the stick

Figure 27. Wooden dolls.

making sure that the doll also has a neck (about 1/2 cm, 1/4"). You can make the neck thicker by winding thick yarn round it.

Little wooden gnome (7 cm, 3")

Wooden doll (3-3 1/2 cm, 1 1/2" high)
Pieces of felt
Textile glue

— Glue a piece of felt to the body and sew up the back. Trim the felt at the bottom.
— Cut out the felt as in Figure 29a. Sew up the back of the hat and glue it to the head.
— Put the collar around the neck and sew it to the front with a few stitches. The points of the collar should remain hanging loosely.

As the heads are so small it is better not to draw a face on them.

Large wooden gnome (11 cm, 4 1/2")

Wooden doll (7 cm, 3" high)
Pieces of felt
Textile glue

This gnome is suitable as a birthday present for a child, and can then be put on the birthday table.

As the wooden doll has a hole in the bottom children can play with it as a finger puppet.

— Dress the gnome as described before, using the pattern in Figure 29b. You can also embroider the gnome's hat.

— Make the beard and hair from unspun wool and glue them on to the head.

— Draw a face with a coloured crayon.

Figure 28. Wooden gnomes.

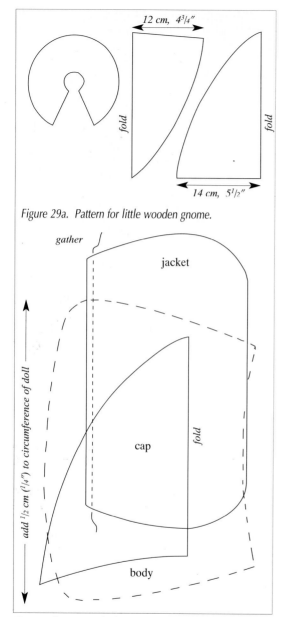

12 cm, 4³/₄"

fold

fold

14 cm, 5¹/₂"

Figure 29a. Pattern for little wooden gnome.

gather

jacket

add ¹/₂ cm (¹/₄") to circumference of doll

cap

fold

body

Figure 29b. Pattern for large wooden gnome.

Rock gnome (11 cm, 4¹/₂")

Wooden doll (about 7 cm, 3" tall)
Pieces of felt (red and two shades of grey)
Unspun sheep's wool or cotton wool

— Cut out the pattern twice in Figure 26b, page 27. Sew the front of the jacket to the darker underpiece leaving about ¹/₂ cm (¹/₄") showing. Repeat with the back. Sew up the two side seams and the bottom of the jacket sleeves. Sew the hands on to the sleeves.
— Put the wooden doll into the jacket and sew up the shoulders and sleeves. The jacket should be longer than the doll.
— Sew the hat together and glue it on to the head. Give the gnome a beard and some hair of wool and draw a face.

Figure 30. Rock gnome.

Gnomes Using Yarn

Woollen yarn gnome (7 cm, 3")

Thick wool yarn in various colours
Thread in various colours
Stiff card

— For the arms wind some woollen yarn about twenty times around a 6 cm (2¼") piece of card. Tie the ends with a piece of thread.

  Remove the wool from the card and tie the hands at about 1 cm (½") from each end (Figure 32).

— For the head, upper and lower parts of the body wind the wool 40 times around an 8 cm (3")

Figure 31. Woollen yarn gnomes.

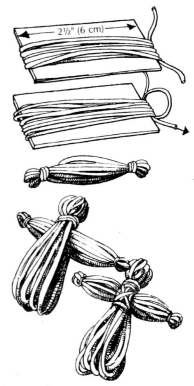

Figure 32. Making a woollen yarn gnome.

piece of card. Tie one end of the wool where the head is to be, and then take the wool off the card. Tie the neck at 2 cm (¾").

— Push the wool for the arms under the neck and through the loop of the upper body. Tie up the waist.

— Divide the wool of the lower loop into two equal parts. Tie the feet and hands at the ends.

Figure 33. Little knitted gnomes.

Little knitted gnomes (10 cm, 4")

Knitting cotton or fine wool
Knitting needles No. 13 (US #1)
Unspun sheep's wool

Body and head
— Cast on 24 stitches and knit 4 rows plain and then 10 rows stocking stitch (1 row plain, 1 row purl). In the eleventh row (plain) knit two stitches together. Knit the remaining twelve stitches of the next row purl (Figure 34).
— Use either pink or beige cotton or wool for the head. Knit 10 rows stocking stitch. In the eleventh row knit every two stitches together. In the next row cast off.
— Fold the knitting in two lengthwise, and sew up the top and back. Fill the head with unspun wool. Stitch a thread around the neck, draw tight and tie it at the back.

Hat
— Cast on 20 stitches and knit two rows plain. Then knit 6 rows stocking stitch. In the seventh row knit the first two and last two stitches together and repeat for the eleventh, thirteenth, fifteenth rows, and so on until all the stitches are finished.
— Sew the sides together and sew the hat firmly on to the head.

Collar
— Cast on 26 stitches and knit 2 rows plain. Then knit 4 rows stocking stitch. In the fifth row knit every two stitches together and cast off the next row (see the collar in Figure 33).
— Sew the collar around the gnome's neck, leaving the front seam open.

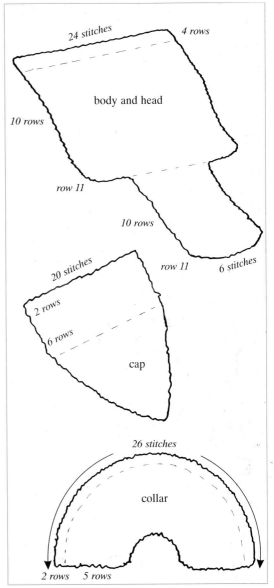

Figure 34. Pattern for little knitted gnome.

Knitted baby gnome (18 cm, 7")

Different coloured knitting wools
Needles No. 10 (US # 4)
Unspun sheep's wool

This little doll is made from a rectangular piece of knitted wool which is then sewn together.

— Cast on 30 stitches and knit 30 rows (15 ridges) plain in red wool. Then knit 8 rows plain in orange wool, 24 rows plain in beige, and another 8 rows in orange. Finally, knit another 30 rows in red. Cast off (Figure 36).
— Fold the piece into two, and sew up the sides, leaving the bottom part open.

Figure 35. Knitted baby gnome

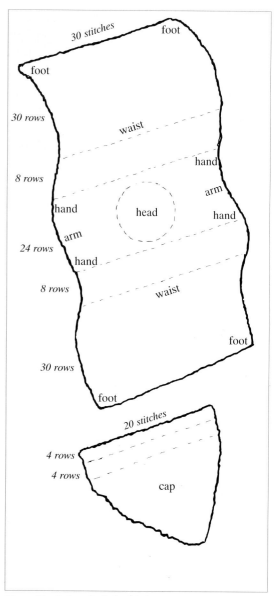

Figure 36. Pattern for knitted baby gnome.

— Take a tuft of unspun wool and fill the middle of the beige part. Make a round ball for the head and tie it up with a beige thread. Tie the thread securely and cut off the ends.

— At each end of the beige piece make a little ball and tie it up for hands.

— Pass an orange thread through the stitches between the orange and red wools. Pull the thread a little to make the waist. The waist should not be too narrow. Fill the upper body with some unspun wool.

— Sew up the middle of the bottom part with a few stitches, leaving an opening for stuffing on either side. Then pass the red thread at the front through the wool stuffing and up to the waist. Push the thread through the body and out at the back. Pass the thread back down again. When you pull the thread tight it will draw the middle up and thus make legs. Tie off the thread.

— Make feet at both ends of the red part and tie them off. Finally fill the legs with unspun wool and sew up the insides of the legs.

Hat
— Cast on 20 stitches of red wool and knit 4 rows plain. Then take orange wool and knit 4 rows plain. Now, in each subsequent row knit the first two stitches together until the stitches are finished.

— Sew up the hat, put it on the head and secure it.

Knitted gnome (30 cm, 12″)

Different coloured knitting wools
Needles No. 10 (US # 4)
Unspun sheep's wool

Body and legs
— Cast on 20 stitches for the left foot.

— Knit 2 rows plain and then make the foot as follows: in rows 3, 5, and 7 after five stitches sew two stitches together. Then do the same in row 9 after 4 stitches, retaining 16 stitches (Figure 38).

— In row 11 change to the colour for the gnome's suit. Knit 18 rows (9 ridges) for the leg. Put this piece aside for a moment.

— Cast on 20 stitches for the right foot and knit 2 rows plain. In row 3, after 13 stitches, knit 2 together. Do the same in row 5 after 12 stitches, and in row 7 and 9 after 11 stitches. In row 11 change over into the new colour and knit 18 rows for the right leg.

— Cast the two legs on to one needle and knit 26 rows (13 ridges) with 32 stitches.

— In the next row, for the shoulders, cast off 4 stitches after 6 stitches. Repeat this after 12 stitches.

— With the remaining 24 stitches knit 17 rows stocking stitch (1 purl, 1 plain) in the colour for the head. In row 18 knit every two together, and with the remaining 12 stitches knit row 19 in purl. In row 20 knit every two together then cast off.

Arms
— For one arm cast on 14 stitches in the colour of the gnome's suit. Knit 14 rows plain. Then with the colour for the hands knit 6 rows stocking stitch. In the next row knit every two stitches together, then knit one last row and cast off. Repeat for the second arm.

Hat

— Cast on 38 stitches and knit 14 rows plain (7 ridges). Then in each row knit the first two stitches together continuing until one stitch remains, then cast it off.

Finishing off

— Sew up the legs and the feet, making the seam below the foot run from the toes to the heel. Stuff the feet firmly with unspun wool and gather the ankles. The legs can be stuffed less tightly.
— Sew up the back, leaving a bit open half-way up for the stuffing. Leave a bit open at the back of the head when sewing this up.
— Stuff a tuft of wool into the neck and gather. Without this tuft the head will not sit properly. Continue to stuff the head and body; the head more firmly than the body.
— Sew up the hands and arms and stuff the hands to make them nice and round. Gather the wrists and then fill the arms. Sew the arms on to the shoulders and sew up 4 stitches of the shoulders.
— Check that the head and body are well stuffed and sew up the openings.
— Sew up the hat. Fill part of the hat and sew it securely on to the head. Then attach the back of it firmly to the shoulders to make it sit correctly.
— Sew the beard and hair (unspun wool) on to the head with embroidery thread and embroider two eyes and a mouth on the face. You can also make eyes by pulling them in with a needle and thread from the back of the head.

Variation

You can also make a head from cotton material for this gnome (see Running Gnome on p. 42).

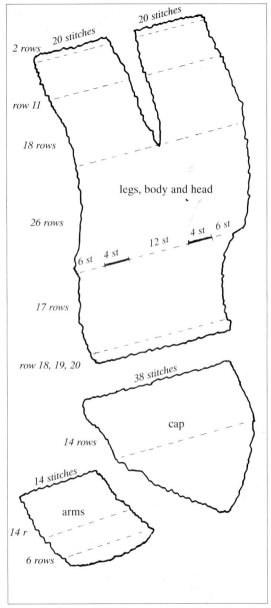

Figure 37. Knitted gnomes.

Figure 38. Pattern for a knitted gnome.

Figure 39. Knitted cotton gnome.

Variation: **Knitted cotton gnome** *(20 cm, 8")*

The gnome in Figure 39 is knitted with the same number of rows as described above. Use needles No. 13 (US # 1)

Knitted puppet (28 cm, 11")

Knitting yarn for body and hat
Skin-coloured wool for head and arms
Darker wool for beard and hair
Needles no 8 (US # 6)

— For the front cast on 30 stitches and knit 48 rows plain in coloured wool. Then knit 28 rows plain with skin-coloured wool. This will eventually form the head and arms. Then knit 48 rows plain for the back in the same colour that you started with.
— Fold the knitted piece and sew up the sides.
— Take a tuft of unspun wool and stuff it against the fold where the head is going to be (Figure 40). Make the head into a round ball and tie with a woollen thread. Do not tie the neck too tightly, so a forefinger can be inserted into the puppet.

Hat
— Cast on 26 stitches and knit 10 rows plain. In each following row knit the first two stitches together until all the stitches are finished.
— Sew up the hat and stuff with a little unspun wool. Sew it securely on to the head.

Hair
— See the description of the Tree Gnome at the bottom of page 26.
— Only when the puppet is quite finished can you start work on the face. You can mark the place where the eyes and mouth are to be by inserting three pins into the head (Figure 60 on p. 58). The eyes should be in the middle of the face. Embroider the eyes and mouth.

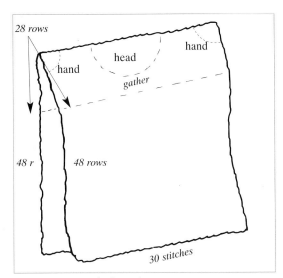

Figure 40. Pattern for knitted puppet.

Figure 41. Knitted puppet.

Story-telling puppet (21 cm, 8″)

Different coloured knitting yarns
Knitting-needles no 10 (US # 4)
Unspun sheep's wool

You can put your fingers into the arms of this puppet, so he can move. You can let him tell a story or talk with the children.

Body and legs
— Cast on 36 stitches for the shoulders. Knit 20 rows ribbed (1 plain, 1 purl). Cast off 8 stitches at each edge and cast them on again in the following row. Knit four more rows, then knit 18 rows with 18 stitches for one leg and cast off. Repeat with the other 18 stitches (Figure 43).

Head
— Pick up the 36 stitches of the shoulders again and knit one row in beige wool. In the following row knit one stitch, then knit two together, knit one, knit two together, and so on.
— Knit 18 rows with the remaining 24 stitches and cast off.

Jacket with hands
— The jacket consists of four parts, a front, a back and two separate arms. For the front cast on 24 stitches and knit 4 rows plain. Then knit 24 rows stocking stitch (1 row purl, 1 row plain) and then round the 4 plain rows knit the two last stitches together. Cast off the 12 remaining stitches.
— Knit the back in the same way.
— For the sleeves cast on 16 stitches and knit two rows plain for the cuffs and then 6 rows stocking stitch. In rows 7 and 9 knit the two first and last stitches together. At row 10 cast off.

39

Figure 42a–42d. Story-telling puppet.

— Knit the hand separately. Cast on 14 stitches and knit 6 rows stocking stitch. In row 7 knit every two stitches together and cast off the remaining 7 stitches.

Pointed hat

— Cast on 36 stitches and knit two rows plain. Then knit stocking stitch. In every fourth row knit the first two and last two stitches together until all the stitches are finished.

Slippers

— Cast on 26 stitches. Knit 4 rows plain. In the following six rows knit all the first and last two stitches together, so that the shape becomes wider.

Finishing off

— Sew the legs together leaving the back open.
— Now sew up the slippers and stuff a little unspun wool into the toes. Pass the slippers over the legs and secure them.
— Fill the legs with unspun wool and sew them up at the top.
— For the knitted head make an inner head' out of material and unspun wool. For this follow stages 1 and 2 on page 55.
— Pull the knitted piece for the head tightly round the material head and secure it at the back and front.
— Fill the upper body loosely with unspun wool and sew up the back seam.
— Sew up the side seams of the jacket. Put the jacket on to the gnome by passing the legs through the neck opening and then sew the shoulder seams.
— Sew up the side seams of the arms and attach the hands. Then sew the front seam of the arms only on to the jacket. Leave the back seam open so that you can insert your fingers.

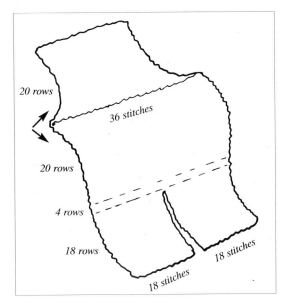

Figure 43. Pattern for the story-telling gnome.

— Sew up the back seam of the pointed hat and secure it to the head.
— Give the gnome a beard and some hair out of unspun wool and embroider the face.

Walking gnome (21 cm, 8")

Different coloured knitting wools
Knitting-needles No. 10 (US # 4)
Unspun sheep's wool
Large safety-pins

Legs and body (Figure 45)
— Cast on 18 stitches for one leg. Knit 18 rows rib (1 stitch plain, 1 purl). On the same needle cast on another 18 stitches for the second leg and then knit another 18 rows rib.
— Now knit both legs together (you will have then 36 stitches). Knit 8 rows.
— Set 8 stitches at each side on a safety-pin and increase the following row with 8 stitches at each edge. Knit 16 rows rib for the upper body and cast off.

Figure 44. Walking gnome.

Arms and jacket
— Cast on 20 stitches and knit 4 rows plain (2 ridges) and then 14 rows stocking stitch.
— On each side increase 8 stitches for the arms. Knit 8 rows stocking stitch except for the first and last two stitches, which you should knit plain to make the cuffs. Knit 15 stitches in the next row, then cast off 6 for the neck opening. Knit the remaining 15 stitches.
— In the next row knit 15 stitches, cast on another 6 stitches, then knit another 15 stitches. Knit 8 rows stocking stitch.
— Cast off 8 stitches on both sides. Knit 14 rows stocking stitch and finally 4 rows plain and cast off.

Hat
— Cast on 36 stitches and knit 4 rows ribbed.
— In every fourth row knit two stitches together at each end. When there are still 14 stitches left over knit two stitches together at each end of every second row until all the stitches are finished.

Boots
— Begin at the soles of the boots. Cast on 26 stitches and knit 4 rows stocking stitch.
— In the following 6 rows knit the first and last two stitches together.
— With the remaining stitches knit a further 8 rows plain (4 ridges) and cast off.

Head and hands
— The head and hands are made of cotton material. For the head see the description, stages 1, 2 and 3, on page 55.
— For the hands take two pieces of cotton about 4 x 4 cm (1½" x 1½") in size. Place a little tuft of wool in the middle and tie a thread around it.

Finishing off

— Fold the sides of the legs and the body inwards. Sew up the inside seams of the legs and the back seam of the trousers (a-a, b-b, c-c).

— Sew up the slippers and stuff a little unspun wool into the toes. Pass the slippers over the legs and secure them.

— Sew up the sleeves and the side seams of the jacket (a-a, b-b, c-c, d-d). Put the hands into the jacket sleeves and secure them. Fill the arms loosely with unspun wool.

— Slip the jacket over the body leaving the back seam of the body open. Push the head through the neck opening of the jacket and secure it to the body. Gather the top of the body. Stuff the body with unspun wool and sew up the back seam of the body.

— Sew the bottom of the back of the jacket on to the front inside of the body, leaving the back of the waist open for your fingers to go into the legs (see Figure 45). The front of the jacket should hang free.

— From each safety pin push the 8 stitches back on to the knitting needles. Knit 10 rows of 16 stitches ribbed in the same colour as the jacket and then cast off. Sew the sides of this piece on to the sides of the jacket to prevent the doll flopping forward.

— Sew up the back seam of the hat and secure it to the head.

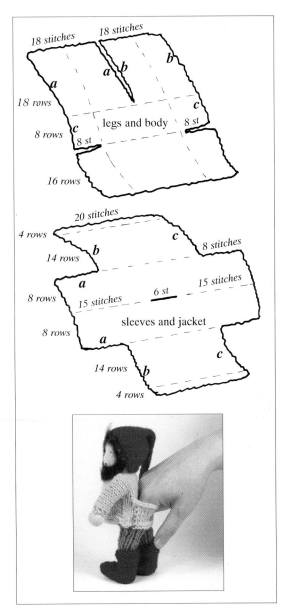

Figure 45. Pattern for walking gnome.

Dolls for Young Children

Baby gnome (28 cm, 11″)

Unspun wool
Pink cotton material, towelling or flannel

Wash the material beforehand so that the doll will not shrink when it is washed later.
— Make the head out of a piece of cotton about 14 x 14 cm (5½″ x 5½″). See page 55 for instructions.
— Enlarge the pattern in Figure 48 to 150%. Cut out the hat and body. Fold with the wrong side of the material inside. Sew up the back of the hat and sew up the round seam with a sewing machine.
— Turn the body right way round by passing the body through the neck opening.
— Stuff the body loosely with some unspun wool. Tie the hands with strong thread.
— Turn the neck opening over by ½ cm (¼″) and gather it in. Put the head into the neck opening. Pull in the gathering thread and fasten it off. Sew the head securely on to the body.
— Gather in the waist just a little.
— Turn the hat right way round, fold one edge of the hat inwards and sew it on to the head.
— If desired you can add some decoration.

Cuddly gnome (30 cm, 12″)

A piece of flannel or other soft material
Unspun sheep's wool
Thin cotton material for the inside of the head
4 beads (diameter about 16 mm, ⅝″)
Ribbon

The teething gnome is a doll for very little children. Make sure that it is firmly stitched together. If you make two identical gnomes you will have one in reserve while the other is being washed.

Figure 47. Cuddly gnome.

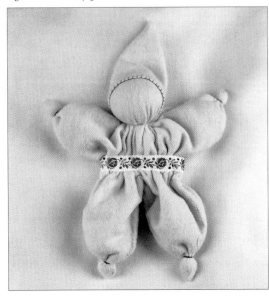

Figure 46. Baby gnome.

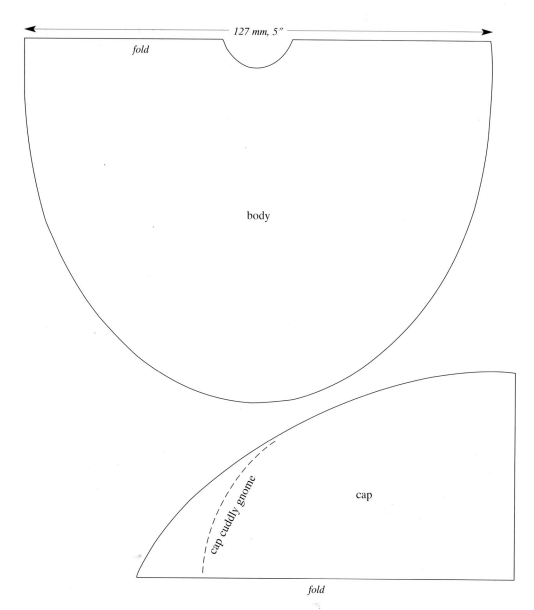

Figure 48. Pattern for a baby gnome (enlarge to 150%).

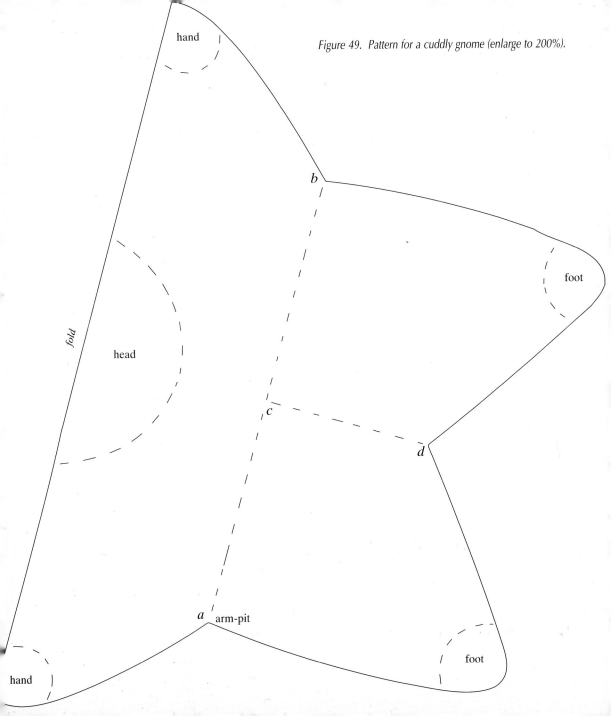

Figure 49. Pattern for a cuddly gnome (enlarge to 200%).

— Wash the material beforehand. It will then be soft and clean and the doll will not shrink when it is washed later.
— Enlarge the pattern in Figure 49 to 200%. Cut out the pattern on the washed material.
— Sew all the seams except one with the sewing machine on the wrong side. Turn the material inside out. Put a bead where the hands and feet are to be, and tie up the material on the outside with red thread.
— Make a head out of a 14 x 14 cm (5½" x 5½") piece of cotton. See the description, stages 1, 2 and 3 on page 55.
— Insert this inner head into the body, and position where the head is to be (see Figure 49). Wrap the material round the inner head and tie it up at the neck with strong thread.
— Stuff a little unspun sheep's wool into the arms and legs and sew up the open seam.
— Gather in the waist a little from a to b, making sure that you do not pull it in too tight. Now gather the material from c to d. In this way you make the legs.
— Sew a pretty ribbon around the waist.
— Cut out the hat as in Figure 48 and sew up the back. Turn the hat inside out. Fold the material ½ cm (¼") in and sew the hat securely on to the head.

Climbing gnome (16 cm, 6½")

Pieces of fabric, plywood (8 mm, ⅜" thick), beads (diameter 16 mm, ⅝"), a stick (about 12 cm, 5" long), paint, varnish, fret-saw, drill (3 mm, ⅛"), nylon cord.

Little children love making this gnome climb up the cord and slide down again.

— Only the upper body with the head and the shoes are made of wood. The legs and the pointed hat are made of material. You can make the whole gnome out of wood, but if the legs and the pointed hat are made of fabric they will shake

Figure 50. Climbing gnome.

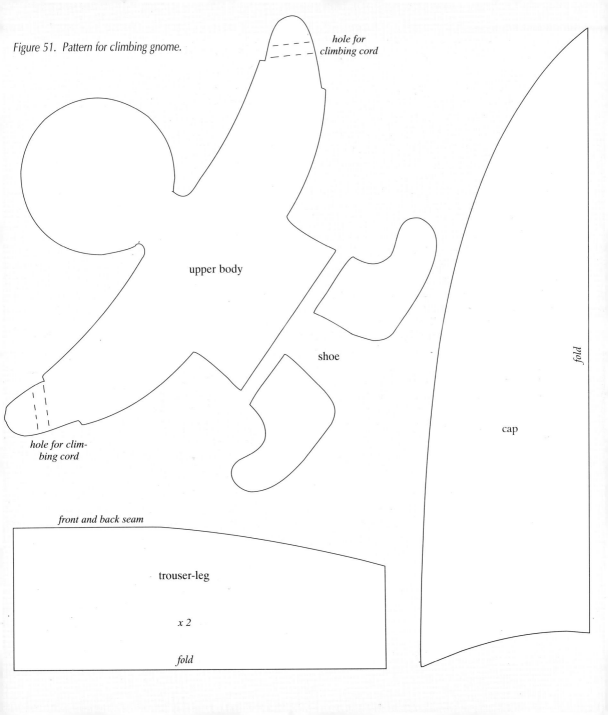

Figure 51. Pattern for climbing gnome.

hole for
climbing cord

upper body

shoe

fold

cap

hole for clim-
bing cord

front and back seam

trouser-leg

x 2

fold

Gnomes with a Wire Frame

about when he climbs. The gnome can climb because the holes in his hands are drilled so that they slant outwards (Figure 51).
— Draw the pattern (in Figure 51) for the upper body and shoes on to a piece of plywood. Cut it out with a fret-saw and sandpaper it smooth.
— Drill two holes (diameter 3mm, 1/8") through the hands angled as in the pattern.
— Paint the jacket, shoes and skin colour of the face on to to the wood. Use poster paints. Paint or draw the details of the face once the background colour is dry, but do not thin down the paint too much, otherwise the colours will run.
— Varnish the painted wood.

— Cut out the hat and trousers from the material. Fold the material with the wrong in and sew the seams of the hat, and the trouser legs.
— Turn the trousers so that the right side is on the outside again. Fold over an edge at the waist and pass a gathering thread through it.
— Glue the trousers on to the wooden upper body and pull in the gathering thread. Fold the bottoms of the trouser legs inwards and glue them firmly to the shoes.
— Turn the hat right side out and glue it on to the wooden head. If required glue a beard on to the face.
— Drill a hole (diameter 3 mm, 1/8") at each end of the stick and one in the centre.
— Finally thread two equal lengths of cord through the stick, hands and beads. Tie the cord with a double knot (Figure 50). When you pull on each of the cords in turn the gnome will climb.

Little folk (22 cm, 8½")

Wire (thickness 1.5 mm, 1/16", length 75 cm, 30")
Carded fleece
Pieces of felt
Unspun sheep's wool
Cotton material
Soft thin cotton material
Embroidery thread
Strong cotton thread (button-thread)
A little bell
Tissues or kitchen-roll
Masking tape

These gnomes are more elaborate than the others in this book. Kindergarten-age children will enjoy playing with them. You can also place these gnomes around the house as decorations.

You will need more time to make these gnomes, especially the Tomten. It would take up too much space to include the patterns for all of the gnomes illustrated here. Start with the patterns given and with experience you will be able to vary the patterns yourself.

The frame
— Bend the wire as shown in Figure 53.
— At the bottom of the wire frame bend the wire to make two feet which will allow the gnome to stand (Figure 54). Make sure that the wire at the bottom is as flat as possible, and check that both legs are of equal length.
— Cut out soles and covers for each foot from a piece of stiff card, one for below and one for

Figure 52. Two forest gnomes.

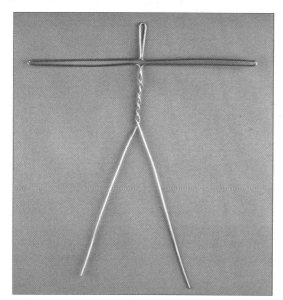

Figure 53. Frame.

Figure 54. Body.

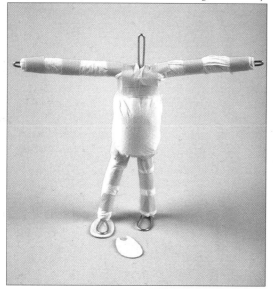

above each foot (Figure 54). Cut out a piece at the ankle of the upper piece so that the wire foot sits properly between the card. Attach the wire to the sole with adhesive tape. Place the upper cover on the wire foot and stick the card pieces together with adhesive tape.

Dressing the frame
— Now you have to fill out the frame by wrapping unspun wool round the arms, body and legs until they are of the required thickness. This is best done layer by layer.

You can also make the body by wrapping tissue paper or kitchen roll around the frame. Take a good length of paper and fold it several times. Wrap it round the frame and secure the paper with masking tape. Begin with the neck, arms and legs. Then move on to the body. Make sure that the gnome gets a good firm belly (Figure 54).

— Once the body is sufficiently filled out with paper you can then (if you wish) clothe it with a thin layer of teased-out wool, as with the Tomten on page 64. Wind some thread around the wool and tie it securely.

Hands
— Cut the hands out from a piece of cotton. As shown in Figure 58 a bit of the lower arm is fastened on to the hand. Sew up the seams, pull the material right way round, and fill the hands with a bit of wool. Pull the piece of lower arm over the arms of the wire frame and secure it.

Figure 55. Reading gnome.

Figure 56a.

Figure 56b.

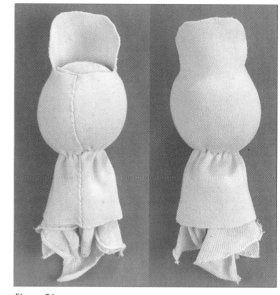

Figure 56c.

Figure 56d.

Feet
— For the feet cut out a piece of material and place it under the card soles. Fold the piece of cotton over the foot and tie it at the top.

The head
1. Roll a good sized tuft of unspun sheep's wool or cotton wool into a ball and lay it on a square of soft thin cotton material, about 16 x 16 cm (6½" x 6½") in size (Figure 56a).
2. Pull the cotton tightly around the ball of wool to make a firm head. Add some wool if the head is too small or does not feel firm enough. Tie the piece at the neck. For simple dolls or very small dolls this will be enough for the head (Figure 56b).
3. In order not to have creases sew a second piece of pink cotton tightly around the head. Make a cut in the top of this second piece and sew it up tightly around the head (Figure 56c). This will take out any crease more effectively.
4. To make a more defined face delineate the eye sockets by winding a thread horizontally around the middle of the head of Figure 56b. Secure the thread with a few stitches at the ears. The result is shown in Figure 56d (where the nose of the next step is also shown).
5. As well as an eye-line you can also make a nose. For this make a little ball of unspun wool and sew it inside a piece of cotton in the correct position (Figure 56d). Shape the nose so that the it is thicker at the bottom.
6. Then sew the second piece of material tightly over the head (see stage 3 and Figure 56c).

— Cut into the material at the side if the neck where the shoulders are to be. Push the head and neck over the wire neck of the frame. Sew the stuffed neck firmly on to the frame. Only add the face and beard when the gnome is finished.

Figure 57. A group of gnomes.

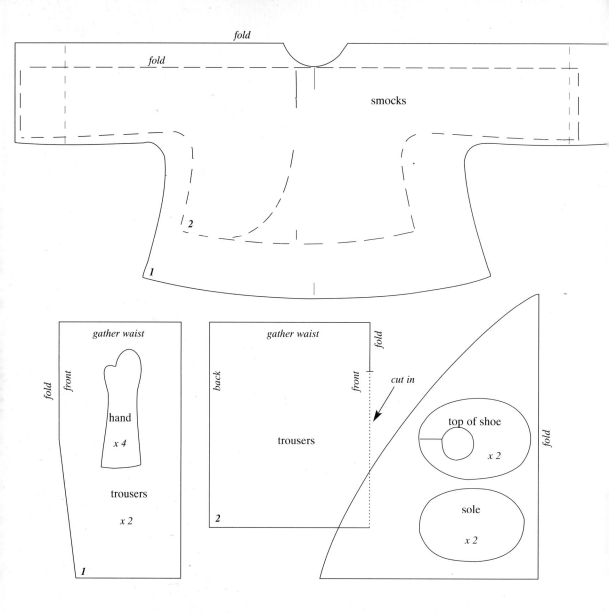

Figure 58. Pattern for little folk (enlarge to 150%).

Figure 59. Two gnomes with their treasures.

Figure 60. Marking the place for the eyes and mouth.

Clothes and shoes

— Make sure that the body, hands and legs are not too thick so that you can sew the loosely-fitting clothes together before you dress the gnome. With the Old Gnome (p. 59) and The Tomten (p. 63) the clothes are sewn around the body.

— Enlarge the pattern in Figure 58 to 150%. Figure 57 shows gnomes with different kinds of clothes. Figure 58 gives two possible patterns. You can decide whether to make a smock, or a jacket opening at the front. Cut out the pattern in felt. Finish off the edges with blanket stitch using embroidery thread. First sew the trousers together. Pass a gathering thread through the top. Put the trousers on and secure them by pulling in the gathering thread and tying it off.

— Sew the jacket together leaving the front open. Put the jacket on and sew up the front with tiny blanket stitches. Secure the trousers and the jacket to the body with a few stitches.

— You can use a thread of different colour to make a decorative border with blanket stitch.

— Make sure that the circumference of the head and the hat are the same size. Cut out the hat and blanket stitch around the edges. Sew the bell on to the end.

— The shoes consist of a sole and an upper part. Cut out the soles a little larger than the feet (see the pattern in Figure 58). Cut a hole into the upper part where the ankle is and cut into the back as well. Sew the upper part on to the sole using blanket stitch. Slip the shoe on to the foot and sew up the back (see Figure 55).

Face

— Give the gnome a beard of unspun sheep's wool or carded fleece. Tease out the wool a little and sew the wool on with tiny stitches. Sew some wool on to the forehead as well, and behind the neck. Then sew the hat on to the head.

— You can mark the position of the eyes and mouth by sticking three pins (with heads) into the head. The eyes should be in the middle of the face although they can perhaps be a little lower (Figure 60). Draw the eyes and mouth with a coloured crayon and give the gnome rosy cheeks.

Old gnome (22 cm, 9″)

Wire (thickness 1.5 mm, ¹/₁₆″)
Carded fleece
Unspun sheep's wool
Cotton material
Soft thin cotton material
Little bell

— Make the frame, hands, feet and head as described on page 50 (see also Figure 61). As you can see in Figure 63 the gnome has a large nose. Step 5 on p.55 and Figure 56d describes how to do this.
— For slippers use a piece of dark cotton on the bottom of the soles. Fold the cotton round the foot and tie securely at the top. You can also make the foot a bit thicker by stuffing in some wool before tying the slipper.
— The hands and shoes of this old gnome are quite big. As the sleeves and trouser legs fit fairly tightly you will have to sew the clothes around the body.
— For clothes use the pattern in Figure 62. Enlarge the pattern to 150%. Use coloured cotton material (old T-shirts are suitable). Cut the clothes out larger than the pattern with a seam of half a centimetre.
— First make the trousers. Fold the seams in and tack them. Place the trousers round the lower body and sew up the seams of the legs and the back using running stitch. Pass a gathering thread along the top of the trousers. Put the trousers on and secure them by pulling in the gathering , thread and securing it. Remove the tacking thread from the trousers.
— Cut open the back of the jacket and finish off as with the trousers.
— Sew the sleeves on to the hands, and the bottom of the jacket on to the trousers.
— Sew the hat together and secure it to the head.

— The deep lying sockets and prominent nose of the gnome call for very distinct eyes. Draw them with coloured crayon or embroider them with embroidery thread.
— Make a beard, a moustache and eyebrows from unspun wool and sew them on.

Figure 61. Body and head of old gnome.

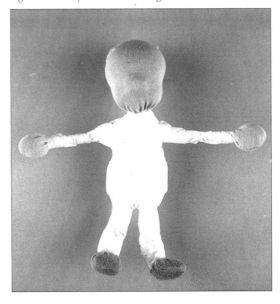

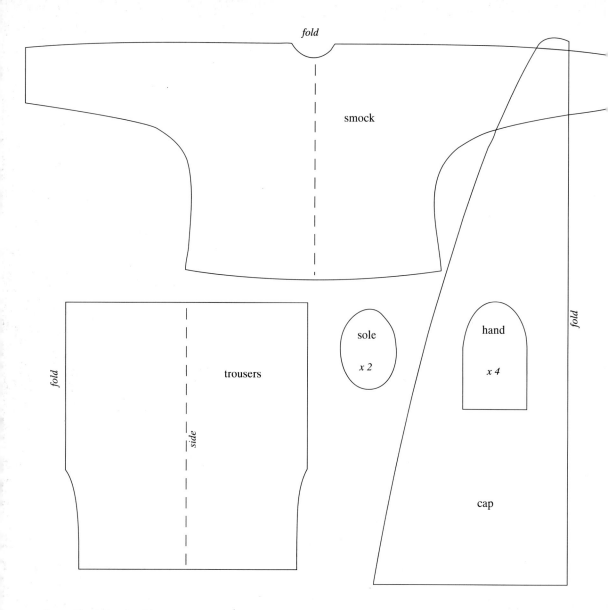

fold

smock

fold

fold

trousers

side

sole

x 2

hand

x 4

cap

Figure 62. Pattern for old gnome.

Figure 63. Old gnome.

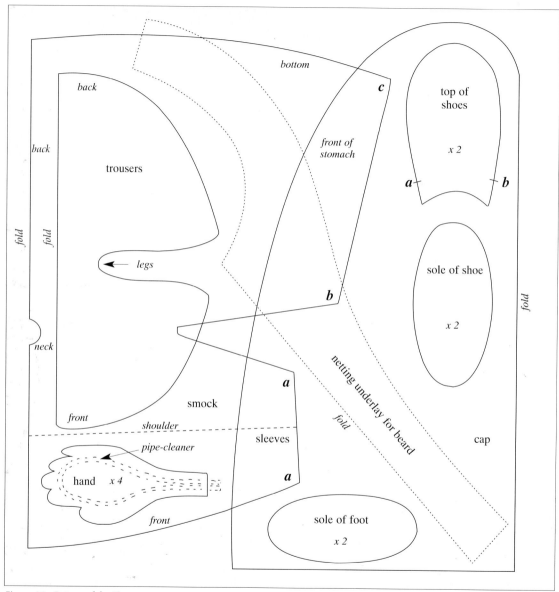

Figure 64. Pattern of the Tomten.

The Tomten (20 cm, 8")

Wood-based modelling paste or
Papiermâché made from toilet paper and starch
Wire
Kitchen roll
Masking tape
Unspun wool
Cotton material
Netting
Polystyrene ball (diameter 5 cm, 2")
Poster paint

The Tomten is a little gnome who lives in remote parts of Sweden on isolated ancient farmsteads. See *The Tomten* and *The Tomten and the Fox* by Astrid Lindgren illustrated by Harald Wiberg (Floris Books).

First make the head; it can dry while you are working on the body. Dress the body completely and then glue the head to the neck, and finally fix the hat and the beard.

Head

Because the Tomten has a big prominent nose and a face with many contours you will have to model the head. Wood-based modelling-paste is ideal, especially as it is not too heavy. Add water to the modelling paste and knead the whole to a firm clay-like mass. Alternatively you can use papiermâché. Tear the toilet paper into little pieces and keep adding it to the starch until it forms a flexible paste which you can mould. Pull the lumps of paper apart.
— Place the polystyrene ball on a stand.
— Completely cover the ball with modelling paste or papiermâché (Figure 65). Do not make this too thick otherwise the paste will drip.

Figure 65. Making the head.

Figure 66.

63

— Add more paste to model the face to the right shape, using a little spatula or knife. With papier-mâché smoothen the face before you let it dry. A characteristic of the Tomten's head is the big prominent nose and large cheeks (Figure 66). The Tomten's mouth and chin are not visible, so they do not need to be worked out.

— Set the head on its stand in a dry place and allow the head to dry for at least 24 hours. Make sure it is not too warm (on a stove, for example) as the head may split.

— Once the modelling paste head is dry you can work on it as if it were wood, and sandpaper it smooth (the papiermâché head cannot be sandpapered). You need only finish the face, as the rest will not be visible.

Dressing the frame
— Make the body according to the instructions on pages 50 and 52. Build up the neck until it is the same thickness as the stick on which the head rests.

— The Tomten has a big round back. Put at least twice as much stuffing into the back as into the front. Because the Tomten's jacket fits round him like a bulging bell, enlarge his paper body by winding some unspun wool round it and secure with thread (Figures 67 and 68).

Figure 67. Making the body.

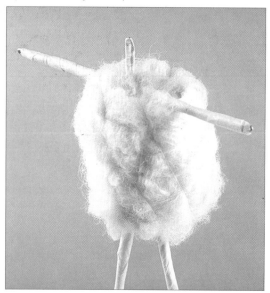

Figure 68. Forming the body.

Figure 69. The Tomten.

Hands, legs and slippers

— Enlarge the pattern in Figure 64 to 150%. Cut out the hands. Bend a pipe-cleaner in two, place the bent end between the top and bottom of the hands and sew them up. Embroider the fingers on the hand. Fill the hands up with unspun wool. Sew them on to the arms (Figure 70).

— The Tomten has very thin, bent legs. These can best be made by winding a darker-coloured wool round them until they are of the required thickness.

— The Tomten's large slippers are sewn straight on to his feet. Cut out the soles and the tops of the slippers and sew them together at points a and b. Put the slippers on to the feet and fill the tops with a little unspun wool. Then sew up the slippers. For the cuffs of the slippers take a piece of felt about 1 cm (½") wide. Sew the cuffs round the ankles and on to the slippers (see Figure 69).

Figure 70. Making the hands.

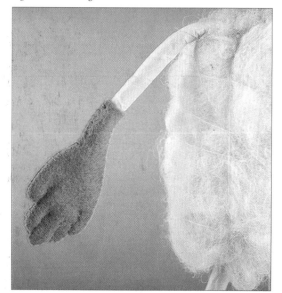

Clothes

— Cut out the clothes of the pattern of Figure 64. Pin the trousers to the body, fold the seams inwards and sew them up.

— Push the neck (without the head) through the neck-opening of the jacket. Fold the sides (b-c) under the arms towards the belly and sew them together. Fold the sleeves around the arms and pin them to start with. Before sewing the sleeves on in front make sure that the jacket fits properly.

— Turn the bottom inwards and gather it in. Pull the thread so that the jacket bulges. If necessary put some more unspun wool at the bottom.

— Sew the hat together and fill it with unspun wool. Tie the end to make a little ball.

Finishing off the head

— Paint the face with poster paint. Cut out some eyes from paper as a trial and draw in the pupils. Position the eyes to the face with pins to get them in the right place. Draw the outline of the eyes on to the face. Remove the paper and paint the eyes. Protect the face with a layer of matt varnish.

— Glue the head on to the neck.

— In order to get the beard into the right shape sew well-teased unspun wool in the shape of the beard on to the netting. Glue the beard on to the face.

Glue the hat on to the head, bringing it down to the eyebrows.

Gnomes Using Other Materials

Gnomes made of nuts

Hazelnuts and walnuts (with shell)
Pieces of felt
Beads
Unspun sheep's wool or cotton wool

These gnomes suitable for the harvest table are easy to make. The larger gnomes have a walnut body and a hazelnut head; the smaller gnomes have a hazelnut for a body and a bead for a head. You can of course make these gnomes from chestnuts or acorns, but they will shrivel up after a time.

The jacket and the hood are in one piece and hold the head and body together.
— Cut out the small or large jacket as in Figure 71, depending on the kind of nut being used, and sew up the back.
— Glue the hood to the forehead and allow the glue to dry properly. Sew the hood under the chin. Stick the bottom of the jacket on to the side of the nut body. Allow the glue to dry thoroughly.

Figure 71. Pattern for a gnome made of nuts.

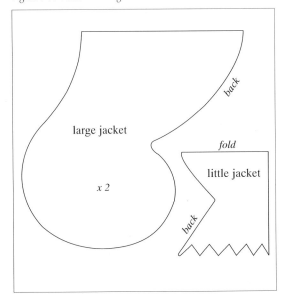

Figure 72. Gnomes made of nuts.

— Gather the material in at the neck.
— Glue a little piece of felt on to a piece of card and cut out the shoes from it. Glue the shoes on to the bottom of the nut. You can also use a bit of beeswax to enable the gnome to stand.
— Give the gnome a beard of unspun wool.

Gnomes made of sticks (about 10 cm, 4")

Sticks (diameter 2-3 cm, 1")
Moss
Unspun wool
Poster paints
Varnish
Saw
Pocket-knife
Sandpaper

Find some fallen branches from trees in the garden, parks or woods. Do not saw them off the trees yourself. Branches with a light-coloured wood and thin bark are the most suitable.

— Choose branches with few knots. The length and thickness of the stick determines how fat or thin the gnome will be. Finish working on the

Figure 74. Preparing the gnomes made of sticks.

Figure 73. Pattern for caps of different diameters of sticks.

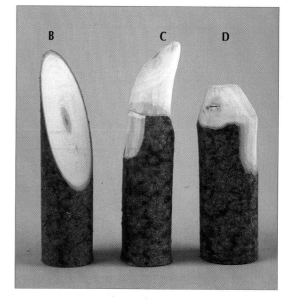

Figure 75. Gnomes made of sticks.

D   C   A   B

head and the hat before you saw off the bottom of the stick. In this way you will have a longer piece of stick to hold while working.

p. 70

— Varnish the gnome as soon as the paint is dry.

Figure 75 shows various gnomes. The simplest is the fire gnome in the centre.
— Take a stick which is not too thick. Cut out a pointed hat at one end.
— With the blade of a knife remove the bark from the place where the face is to be.
— Paint the hat and paint in the eyes and mouth of the face.

You can also make a gnome simply from an obliquely sawn off branch (on the right in Figure 75).
— First saw off the branch obliquely and sandpaper it smooth.
— Then saw off the bottom squarely (Figure 74, left).
— With some white paint paint a beard and a hat on the oblique surface and draw the face.
— Varnish the face and the gnome is finished.

Another gnome has a hat which is worked round with a pocket knife (Figure 75, left of centre). This can be done at home with a rasp or file.
— Remove the bark from the place where the face is to come. For the beard use a bit of moss.

You can also make gnomes with a felt hat (Figure 75, left).
— Cut one end of the stick off obliquely. Carve the face out of the bark.
— The height of the hat should be in keeping with the thickness of the branch. Figure 73 shows patterns for the pointed hat for different diameters of the stick. The smallest circle belongs to the smallest hat.

Gnome transparencies (26 cm, 10")

Scissors or knife with a sharp point
Coloured card
Coloured tissue paper
Grasses, twigs or dried flowers

These transparencies can be hung on the window. The examples given here with grasses and different coloured tissue paper can be varied.
They are not difficult to make and can serve as little presents.

— Mark the outer edge of the transparency on the card.
— Draw in the picture wish to make in such a way that all remaining card will still be attached to the edge. Cut out everything around the picture. For children it is often easier to cut out a shape first, and to stick it on to the back of the frame.

Transparency with coloured tissue paper
— Enlarge the drawing in Figure 77 or make your own design.
— Cut away the spaces between the gnomes, between the hats etc. with a sharp knife. Figure 76 shows clearly the parts which have to be cut away.
— Apply a little glue to the back of the card and stick some pale blue tissue paper over the whole of the back. Make sure that the tissue paper is firmly stuck to the edges.
— At the back cut away the pale blue tissue paper in the places where you are going to stick another colour and stick that colour there. Cut away any superfluous tissue paper. The wider the bits of card are, the easier it is to stick on the tissue paper. However, with narrower lines you can obtain some lovely effects.

Figure 76.

Figure 78.

Figure 77.

Figure 79.

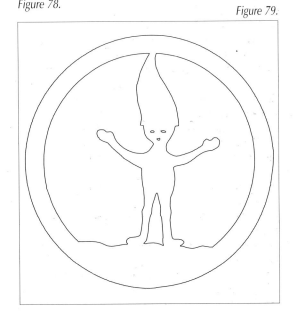

71

Transparency with grasses
See Figures 78 and 79 for an example of this kind of transpatency.
— Stick white tissue paper or tracing paper on the back of the transparency.
— Collect some grasses and stick them at the front at the bottom of the frame with adhesive tape.
— Cut out a shape in card to cover the place where the grasses are attached.

— Cut out more strips in the same way and stick them together until the decoration is long enough.
— Pass a thread through the middle of longer festoons to prevent them from tearing in the middle when they are hung up.

Paper chains

Coloured paper

You will need a number of strips of coloured paper to make this decoration long enough.

— Cut out some strips of paper about 12 cm (5") wide (or high). The length of the strips depends on the size of paper. Fold them concertina fashion into a pack to the width of the figure.
   The two decorations at the top of Figure 81 are 5 cm (2") high and the one at the bottom is 7 cm (3") high.

— As a guide draw a gnome from Figure 81 on a piece of stiff paper the size of the folded pack. The feet and the hands should reach the edge (Figure 80). Cut the gnome out of the paper. This will give you a stencil.
— Draw the outline of the stencil on the folded pack. Cut the shape out of the pack, making sure that you do not cut through the hands and feet where they are attached to the sides. When you open out the pack you will see how the gnomes are holding hands.

Figure 80. Cutting out the gnome for the paper chain.

Figure 81. Paper chains.

Embroidered Gnomes

Table runner (11 cm, 4¹/₂")

*Aida or embroidery cloth (11 cm, 4¹/₂" wide, 6
cross stitches per cm), embroidery thread in
red, orange, pink, pale yellow, dark yellow,
grey, beige, light green, mid-green, dark
green, moss green, pale blue, mid-blue.*

— Aida cloth is obtainable with or without a scal-
loped edge (ornamental edge)
— Start embroidering 4 cm (1¹/₂") from the left
edge and in the sixth hole from the bottom (or the
ornamental edge).

— Work with two threads of embroidery thread.
Each space in Figure 83 takes one cross stitch (or
one tacking stitch for stems of flowers).
— Embroider the second gnome as a mirror
image of the first (Figure 82).
— Make the table runner of the gnomes as long
as you wish.
— You can vary the colours of the gnomes indef-
initely.
— Instead of a table decoration you might like to
hang the runner above the child's bed or above
the chest of drawers.

Figure 82. Embroidered table runner.

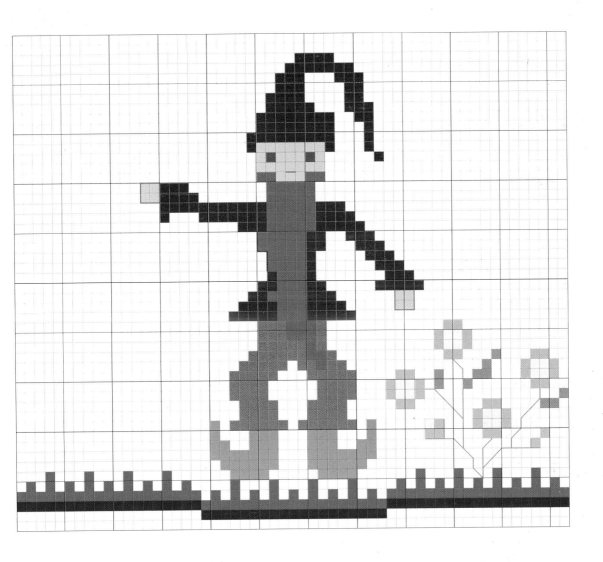

Figure 83. Pattern for table runner.

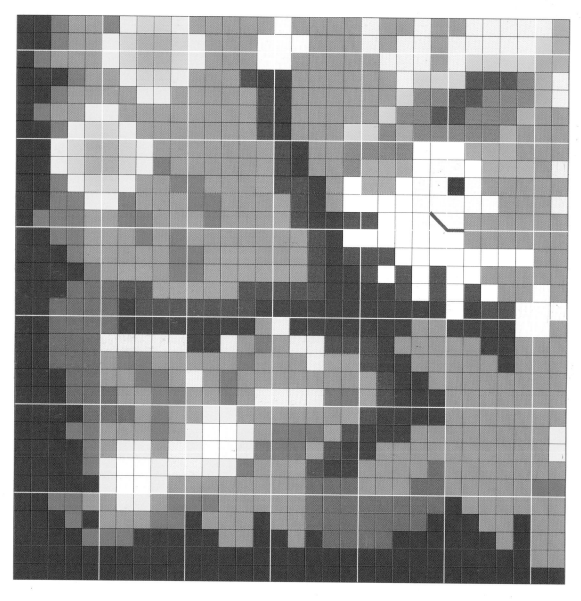

Figure 84. Pattern for embroidered cushion.

Figure 85. Embroidered cushion.

Cushion

Emboidery canvas (45 x 45 cm, 18" x 18", 2 crosses per cm), embroidery wool or thick knitting wool in pale yellow, dark yellow, orange, dark rose, peach-red, dark red, light brown, red-brown, brown, pale green, mid-green, green, dark green.

— Starting from the centre of the canvas, count out the squares of pattern of Figure 84. Each square corresponds to one cross stitch. The design represents one quarter of the cushion. Mark the edges.

— Begin in one corner and embroider in cross stitch. Do not pull the thread too tight.

— The finished cushion will be about 35 x 35 cm (14" x 14"). Begin with dark green and embroider the edge of the cushion. Work with each colour moving towards the middle until the cushion is finished.

— Cut away the extra fabric leaving an unembroidered edge of about 2 cm (³/₄"). Fold the edges in.

— Sew the embroidery on to a cushion cover or pillow case of about 35 x 35 cm (14" x 14") in size.

Wall hanging (50 x 50 cm, 20" x 20")

Background cloth
Felt and/or flannel in various colours
Viline
Embroidery thread

A wall hanging is a nice decoration for a child's room. Sometimes older children can to make it and sew simple forms on to the background.

— It is important to design the composition first and then sew everything on.

— Take a piece of tapestry cloth for the background. Make the trees and grass from felt or flannel. Flannel is stiffer and does not crease so easily when spread on the Viline.

— Cut out the large areas such as the grass, tree trunk, leaves and pine trees. Lay them on the base and move them around until they look right. Tack the areas with a few large stitches on to the base.

— Enlarge the pattern in Figure 87 to 200%. Cut out the gnomes and animals and distribute them over the wall hanging. The gnomes in the foreground are larger than those in the background. Tack the figures to the cloth. Cut out the sun, clouds, flowers and birds and secure these also with a tacking-stitch.

— Now sew on all the parts with button hole stitch, beginning with the grass and the trees.

— Embroider the faces of the gnomes and make the beards from unspun wool

— Finish off the wall hanging by embroidering flowers and grasses.

— Fold the edges of the fabric to the back and sew them up with little stitches. You can make the wall-hanging stiffer by sewing lining material to the back. By passing a stick through the top and bottom seams, or by making loops at the top you can then hang it up.

Figure 86. Wall hanging.

Figure 87.